Dressage for Beginners

Dressage for Beginners

R. L. V. ffrench Blake

With Illustrations by Richard Scollins

HOUGHTON MIFFLIN COMPANY BOSTON

First American edition 1976

Library of Congress Cataloging in Publication Data

ffrench Blake, R   L   V
  Dressage for beginners.

  Bibliography: p.
  1. Dressage. 2. Dressage tests. I. Title.
SF309.5.F47   798'.23   76–11725
ISBN 0–395–24373–4
ISBN 0–395–24399–8 pbk.

Printed in the United States of America

M 10 9 8 7 6 5 4 3 2

Introduction

SINCE the end of World War II in 1945, interest in horses and the sports connected with them has grown at a great pace throughout the United States. Activities once associated with only the very wealthy or with the United States Cavalry have become commonplace among middle-income people.

This has been particularly true with the interest in dressage. An almost unknown term among American horsemen until the decade of the 1950s, interest in dressage as both a method of training and as a competitive sport has increased very rapidly in the past twenty years. There now exist more than three dozen dressage societies or associations in every part of the country concerned with assisting their members in gaining good instruction and in promoting dressage competitively. These have recently been joined together in a national organization called the United States Dressage Federation with over four thousand individual members. Dressage also forms a basic part of the training of the United States Pony Clubs with over ten thousand active members, and increasingly, those interested in show jumping, show hunters, 4-H, equitation competition, and other varieties of equestrian sport are turning to the classical methods of dressage as a means of improving their horses and their riding ability. The Dressage Committee of the American Horse Shows Association, the national equestrian federation of the United States, is the body responsible for the regulation of dressage competition in America in line with the rules of the Fédération Equestre Internationale with headquarters in Brussels.

But while the interest in dressage has grown at a rapid pace, the development of well-trained dressage instructors has not, and each year finds the need for sufficient instructors and trainers to meet the demand greater and greater. There has long been a cry for a good book on basic dressage, one which would provide an introduction to dressage as both a method of training and an equestrian competition, a guide to instructors as well as to riders.

R. L. V. ffrench Blake provided such a book for a similar need in Great Britain with the publication of his *Dressage for Beginners* in 1973. The book was popularly received in Britain and found a ready audience among adults and young riders alike in the United States, but its availability to the American public remained limited. Thus Colonel ffrench Blake has prepared an American edition, revised to make reference to American dressage tests and to reflect American terminology or points of view that differ from those of the British.

Well written and illustrated and aimed at the non-professional Pony Club, 4-H, or riding club instructor as well as at the novice rider, it is a useful book by a horseman with great experience in the training of dressage horses and riders and a keen knowledge and understanding of dressage as a competitive sport.

John H. Fritz, Chairman,
American Horse Shows Association
Dressage Committee

Preface

It is a great honor for me to have this book published in the United States of America. In the preface to the original edition in 1973 I wrote: "For some twenty years, I have been concerned in judging, teaching, watching, and riding dressage. In every novice competition there always seem to be a few who appear not to know what they are trying to do; it is to them that this book is addressed, as well as to those who have not yet started 'doing dressage,' but who for one reason or another, are going to get involved with the art.

"This little book may help them to know what it is all about and on what lines they should start work.

" 'He who does not know the aim, cannot know the way.' "

My feeling that a book for beginners was required has been reinforced by wide circulation in Great Britain, special editions in New Zealand, Australia, Holland, Sweden, and now America.

Since the original edition was written, the F.E.I. "Rules for Dressage" have been revised and retranslated. These revisions have been incorporated into this edition, and the book has been changed as far as possible to include American practice and tests.

However, as I have never been to the United States, I feel it would be presumptuous to attempt to lay down the law on matters American. I have therefore included many parallel references to practices in Great Britain that may be of interest to my American readers and of use to anyone who may be coming over to ride in this country.

Difficulties may arise over language, and I am relying on my kind American advisers, Mrs. Ruth K. Hapgood of Houghton Mifflin Company and Mr. John H. Fritz, Chairman of the American Horse Shows Association Dressage Committee, to keep me on the right lines. For instance, in Great Britain most people refer to the lateral flexion of the horse as "the bend," reserving the word "flexion" for the vertical flexion of the head and neck at the poll. I have also often retained terms such as "Novice" horse that are self-explanatory, rather than always using the American classification of "First Level," and so on. The glossary of terms at the end of the book may help the reader.

I am grateful to Messrs. Methuen and Company for permission to quote from and to adapt some of the drawings from Wilhelm Müseler's *Riding Logic*. I received much help and good advice from leading exponents of dressage in Britain — Mrs. Molly Sivewright and Mrs. Joan Gold, and the former National Instructor, Colonel Bill Froude. Richard Scollins, my illustrator, though no horseman himself, has shown great patience and skill in turning my own crude sketches into accurate and instructive pictures. He is now engaged in illustrating my next book — *Elementary Dressage* — which takes the rider from First to Second Level.

V ff B

Midgham Park Farm, Woolhampton

Contents

Illustrations

Dressage for Beginners

Chapter 1

The Requirements

THERE ARE TWO SIDES TO DRESSAGE — the preparation of the horse, according to a set of well-established principles; and the presentation of the horse, from time to time, before judges, in competition.

This second element — the dressage "test" — is incidental to the first. What matters is the work of rider and horse; the test will help to show progress, establish standards, and subject the rider's methods and their results to informed and expert examination. Without the tests, the rider will be working in a vacuum, without ambition or a target for his or her efforts.

There are many definitions of dressage, but since we are to work toward satisfying an official panel of judges, we will take the official definition (recently rewritten) by the international equestrian authority (the F.E.I.). It can be found in the rules published by the National Federation of the rider's own country — e.g., the British Horse Society or the American Horse Shows Association.

Their definition gives the object of dressage as:

1. Harmonious development of the physique and ability of the horse. As a result it makes the horse calm, supple, loose and flexible, but also confident, attentive and keen, thus achieving perfect understanding with his rider.
2. These qualities are revealed by:
   a. Freedom and regularity of the paces.
   b. Harmony, lightness and ease of the movements.

c. Lightness of the forehand, and engagement of the hind-quarters, originating in a lively impulsion.

d. The acceptance of the bridle, with submissiveness throughout, and without any tension or resistance.

3. The horse thus gives the impression of doing of his own accord what is required of him. Confident and attentive, he submits generously to the control of his rider, remaining absolutely straight in any movement on a straight line, and bending accordingly when moving on curved lines.

4. His walk is regular, free and unconstrained. His trot is free, supple, regular, sustained and active. His canter is united, light, and cadenced. His quarters are never inactive or sluggish; they respond to the slightest indication of the rider, and thereby give life and spirit to all the rest of his body.

5. By virtue of a lively impulsion and the suppleness of his joints, free from the paralyzing effects of resistance, the horse obeys willingly and without hesitation, and responds to the various aids calmly and with precision . . .

6. In all his work, even at the halt, the horse must be on the bit. A horse is "on the bit" when the hocks are correctly placed, the neck is more or less raised, according to the stage of training, and he accepts the bridle with a light and soft contact, and submissiveness throughout. The head should remain in a steady position, as a rule slightly in front of the vertical, with a supple poll as the highest point of the neck, and no resistance should be offered to the rider.

The definition then goes on to give in detail the requirements for the different paces and all the movements, from the basic paces up to the most advanced stages.

The general definition given above is a most carefully phrased statement — every word is of significance, and the students of dressage cannot read it too often, nor should they neglect the detailed definitions of the particular movements which follow in the rule book.

What is your image of dressage? An arena of white boards and letters with an interminable series of the Pony Club or

Training Level novices plodding round all day? — the compulsory ordeal that Combined Training competitors must undergo before they can do their jumping and cross-country? — the classical but sometimes archaic teamwork of the Spanish Riding School or the Cadre Noir? — the theatrical performances of an Oliveira or of a Peralta at the great indoor shows?

In fact, all these are part of the same art; one stage of training leads to another, and riders may go as far on the road to perfection as they want and as ability of rider and horse permits.

The tests issued by the National Federations fall into the following standards: in Britain — Preliminary, Novice, Elementary, Medium, and Advanced. The last named is divided into Prix St. Georges, Intermediate, and Grand Prix (all international tests).

In the United States the categories are: Training Level, First, Second, Third, Fourth Level; Prix St. Georges, Intermediate, and Grand Prix.

Broadly speaking, the additional requirements at each level are as follows:

U.S.	British	Requirements
Training Level	Preliminary	Basic paces, free walk, circles of 20 meters diameter.
		Progressive transitions (i.e., from trot to halt through a few strides of walk).
First Level	Novice	Serpentines at trot
		Lengthened strides at trot
		10 meter circles at trot (U.S.)
		15 meter circles at trot (G.B.)
		Lengthened strides at canter (U.S.)
		Transitions less progressive.

U.S.	British	Requirements
Second Level	Elementary	10 meter circles at trot Shoulder-in (U.S.) 10 meter circles at canter (U.S.) Half-pirouette at walk (U.S.) Simple change of leg through walk (in U.S. through trot only)
	Advanced Elementary	Collected trot and canter (G.B.) Shoulder-in (G.B.) 10 meter circles at canter (G.B.) Medium trot and canter (G.B.) Transitions direct from canter to walk, etc.
Third Level	Medium and advanced medium	Collected walk, trot, and canter Medium trot and canter Extended trot and canter Counter canter 20 meters diameter Rein-back Half-pass and renvers (haunches-in) at trot Voltes (circles of 6 meters) at trot Single flying changes (G.B.)
Fourth Level	Advanced	Trot zig-zags at half-pass (counter-change of hand) Canter serpentine with flying changes, half-pirouettes at canter, four-time flying changes
Prix St. Georges		Counter-canter serpentines or circles of about 15 meters, canter zig-zags at half-pass with flying changes
Intermediate		Canter pirouettes, four, three and two-time flying changes, piaffer with slight forward movement
Grand Prix de Dressage		One-time flying changes, piaffer, and passage

The American Horse Shows Association publish in their rules an admirable table of movements required at the different levels, showing in detail all movements and transitions at every level.

It is interesting to note that the progression in the two countries is very similar, but in the United States smaller circles are introduced at an earlier stage, and the horse is expected to be generally more supple — no bad principle! In the United States the large arena, 60 × 20 meters, may be used at *all* levels, whereas in Great Britain only the small arena is used in all tests, until Medium (Third Level) is reached.

The first three stages (Training Level and Levels 1 — 2) contain the basic requirements of schooling for every form of riding horse, whatever the purpose for which it is to be used; Medium (Third Level) standard is for the rider who needs an intensely active and supple horse, e.g., Three-Day Event horses, polo ponies, show jumpers. Advanced dressage is a specialized art, and the horse that reaches this stage will probably not be used for anything else.

This book is concerned only with helping the beginner to enter on the first stages.

Let us pause then to extract from the complicated language of the definition the bare essentials with which to begin our work on the horse. The rider may have a young, untouched, or "green" horse, or more likely a "spoilt" horse, wrongly schooled by other, less knowledgeable riders. Almost certainly he is a "puller," neck upside-down, one-sided, with one or more bad habits well ingrained. It makes little difference; it is better to start from the beginning in either case. The horse is a creature of habit, and the instilling of good habits can overlay and eradicate bad ones. In any case, dressage involves not only controlling the behavior of the horse but also developing the correct muscles, and allowing muscles incorrectly used to waste away. An example of this is the neck; a pulling horse normally adopts this attitude — head too high and "above the bit"; a bulge of muscle, in the front of the lower part of the neck, is used to resist all efforts of the rider to lower the horse's head or to reduce speed.

Fig. 1. An unschooled horse

Fig. 2. Relaxing the lower muscles of the neck

Make the experiment of standing at the horse's head and lowering it into the correct position by offering him a handful of food. With the other hand feel the muscle at the front of the neck, which will be quite soft and relaxed.

Now, if the horse can be persuaded (not forced) to carry his head in this position, the bulge of muscle, no longer permanently in tension, will gradually atrophy and fade away to its proper proportions, and the horse will be not only better-looking but will also have a much better "mouth."

The essential first steps in training the horse are:

1. Relaxation
2. Free forward movement
3. Correct gait, with regular rhythm, at each pace
4. Straightness

Later will come:

5. Suppleness — correct bends
6. Attitude — including head carriage
7. Improvement of the basic paces or gaits

And later still:

8. Cadence
9. Collection

We will consider each of these steps in turn in the following chapters.

Chapter 2

Starting Work

BEFORE STARTING WORK the rider must have the right equipment. Training and First Level dressage is performed in a plain snaffle, with either cavesson or dropped noseband; no martingale is allowed; a whip may be carried in Britain except in Combined Training competitions, but is not allowed in competitions in the United States. A list of permissible types of snaffle is given in the rules. A long dressage whip is essential for schooling, since it can be applied without taking the hands off the reins.

It is impossible to sit correctly in the wrong saddle; most old-fashioned hunting saddles put the rider too far back. If possible, get a modern type of saddle in which the rider sits comfortably in the lowest part of the seat. The waist of the saddle should also be narrow, allowing the rider to have a "deep" seat, and thus a close feeling of the horse.

We will not yet need an arena, though a confined space is useful, and if there is no access to a covered school or enclosed *manège,* the rider can mark out a rectangle, preferably rather larger than the standard small arena of 40 meters (44 yards) × 20 meters (22 yards). Pegs or oil drums can define an area of flat ground about 60 × 30 yards.

We now come to the question of the rider's seat. This cannot be learned by reading, though an indication of what is required will be found in many textbooks. One of the clearest and most explicit descriptions can be found in Wilhelm Müseler's *Riding Logic* (Methuen).

The only real answer is to go to a good instructor and get

Various types of seat are shown below:

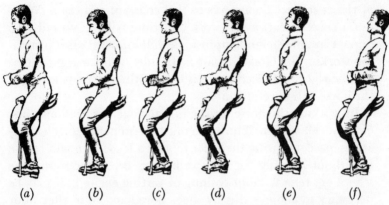

(a)   (b)   (c)   (d)   (e)   (f)

Fig. 3. (a) Leaning forward on the fork. (b) Slack back — head poked forward. (c) Correct — upright, riders' center of gravity balanced over that of the horse. (d) Back braced — correct for driving forward, or in downward transitions. (e) Stiff back — bottom sticking out. (f) Leaning back, reins too long.

To which we may add some local variations:

Fig. 4. (g) "Hunting seat" — lower leg thrust forward. (h) "Cavalry crouch" — rounded back. (i) Weight on the back of the saddle. (j) Show jumping stance, above the saddle, standing on stirrups

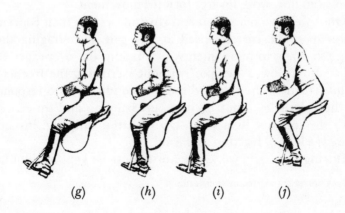

(g)   (h)   (i)   (j)

your seat put right. From time to time go back to check that you have not acquired bad habits. Even the most experienced of riders subject themselves to this constant criticism. Without a correct seat, much work and time will be wasted. To quote Captain Stefan Skupinski, a well-known Polish instructor working in Great Britain: "If rider will be right, horse will be right." The converse is true, if the rider sits wrongly, the horse will develop faults.

In working the horse for the initial stage, we shall aim first of all at relaxation. The horse must be prepared to go calmly at any pace, allowing the rider to give a loose rein and retake it without altering pace, to walk, trot, or canter round the school or arena without rushing or getting excited. It may be necessary to achieve this by sheer boredom, hour after hour of persuading the excitable* horse that he is not going anywhere else, that he is not to be upset by other horses passing by, or by strange sights and sounds. *Until this state of relaxation is achieved, it is no use attempting anything else.* With relaxation will come the second most important factor, a steady rhythm. That is to say, the feet at any pace will come to the ground with the regularity of a metronome, in four-time at the walk (one-two-three-four) ; two-time (one-two, one-two) at the trot; and three-time at the canter. The rider's own rhythm must be as steady as that of his mount, or he may unbalance the horse, as yet unstable.

We can now work for free forward movement.

Once we have relaxation and rhythm, we can then concentrate upon the correct speed at any gait, encouraging the sluggish horse to more energy, persuading the over-eager to drop into a slower "tempo," without sacrificing the freedom of movement. The sluggard must be conditioned to respond to the rider's leg — not by incessant banging and squeezing with the leg, but by a sharp tap with the whip the instant there is a lack of reaction to the aid.

During this early work, the horse must be kept straight at

* Many horses are excited by over-feeding.

all times, particularly during the transitions from one pace to another, and when halting. The rider must not halt or reduce speed by merely pulling on the reins, but by sitting "with" the horse, driving a little on to the bit, and carrying out the transition almost by thinking about it, rather than by any violent application of the aids. In "downward" transitions — canter to trot, trot to walk — the rider must brace the back to avoid tipping forward at the change of pace.

When working in Britain, Colonel Podhajsky, a former head of the Spanish Riding School, was asked to give lessons to some riders with novice horses. "Take them away" he would say; "Go out into the country and work the horse on straight lines, responding properly to the leg. I can teach nothing until that has been done."

One sees many horses in dressage competitions pulling against the rider, cantering far too fast, fighting into the halts and downward transitions. One longs to ring the bell and say "take it away, and come back when you can trot and canter quietly round the arena on a loose rein."

When the horse is moving forward freely, rhythmically, and relaxed, we can consider the next stage, which is to teach the horse to move in curves, accepting a bend to right and left. For this we can start using the arena. Naturally we shall not confine all our work to the enclosure, but will alternate with rides on the road or in the country. Otherwise horse and rider will soon become stale. In addition, riding in the open will take us over rough ground, up and down hills, and into places where the horse will learn to balance himself under the weight of the rider.

Chapter 3

Using the Arena

In britain for novice tests we always use the small arena, which consists of two squares of 20 meters forming a rectangle 40 × 20 meters.

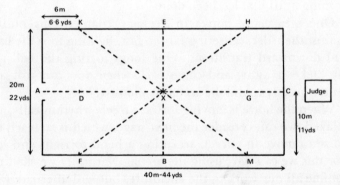

Fig. 5 (a). The small arena

The center line is marked AC, the half-markers on the long sides are E and B, and there are four markers at 6 meters from the end of the long sides, KHMF, marking the diagonals across the school, and also defining the straight length of the long side. Normally, the rider should not start to turn the corner until after passing these markers. The center is marked by X, and the points on the center line at 6 meters from the ends are D and G.

The arena may be marked by continuous or intermittent boards. Entry and exit is by an opening at A — *never* over the boards.

To construct a simple arena, see Appendix 1.

All tests start with an entry at A, a halt and a salute usually at X, followed by a move-off to C, where the rider "tracks" right or left round the arena, "on the right or left rein."

The large or standard arena consists of a rectangle of 60 × 20 meters.

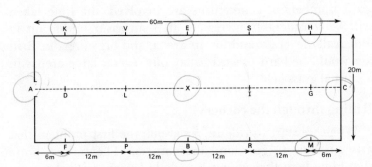

Fig. 5 (b). The large or standard arena

The marks FAK, HCM, and D and G are placed in the same positions as in the small arena, and EXB still indicates the center points lengthways. The intermediate points VS, RP, and LI halve the distances between the main markers, and are 12 meters apart.

Prolonged research has failed to discover by whom, how, where, or why this strange selection of letters originated!

The F.E.I. rules lay down that the center line and the letters D, X, and G should be clearly marked "without however being of such a nature as to frighten the horses." On a grass arena the line can be mown shorter; or a thin line marked with creosote will be clearly visible and will last well. White paint tends to make the horses jump the line. In a sand arena the center line should be raked for each competitor.

If the center line is clearly indicated, it makes matters far easier for both riders and judges during the test, and the line should certainly be marked for schooling purposes. In Britain as in the United States much of our dressage takes place in ordinary grass fields. A well-mown track and center line greatly improves the appearance of the arena and makes for better riding.

The use of the large or standard arena for earlier tests is certainly desirable from the training point of view, but if great numbers of competitors are involved, the time taken will be considerably increased: it is surprisingly difficult to find really level ground for an arena, and organizers in Britain would be hard pressed to lay out several large arenas in a normal grass field.

Riding through the corners

When we start to ride in the arena, the first problem that arises is how to go round the corners. The trained horse should be bent throughout his whole length, to fit the curve on which he is traveling.

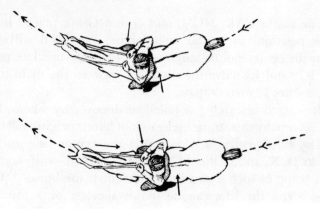

Fig. 6. Riding in a curve

The inside rein supported by a yielding outside rein bends the neck; the rider's outside leg, drawn a little back, bends the quarters round the inside leg — or if you like — the inside leg pushes the center outward. The effect should be to ensure that the track of the hind legs follows exactly in that of the forelegs. The outside rein supports and controls the speed.

Obviously, a stiff horse cannot bend as much as a supple one, and therefore cannot describe so small a circle. All corners should be ridden as a quarter circle, and the rider should go only as deep into the corner at any pace as can be managed without losing the rhythm.

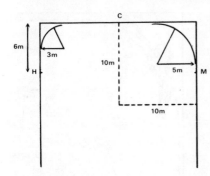

Fig. 7.
Riding through the corners

A fully trained horse, at advanced standard, can canter collected through a corner on a radius of 3 meters, — the quarter of a circle of 6 meters in diameter — as above, left. Above right is a corner on a 5 meter radius, i.e., part of a 10 meter circle.

A good novice horse should be able to walk deep into the corner at 3 meter radius, trot at 5 meter radius, and canter at 6 meter radius thus:

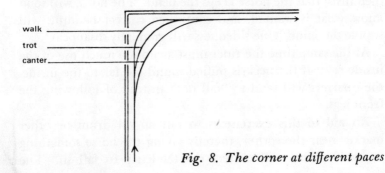

Fig. 8. The corner at different paces

At first this will probably not be possible, since the green horse and the "spoilt" horse will probably not accept the bend at all. When the rider goes round the corner, the horse will "fall in," that is, drop its shoulder inward, and look outward; when the rider tries to establish the bend the horse will leave the track inward. Generally, he will be stiffer on one side than on the other.

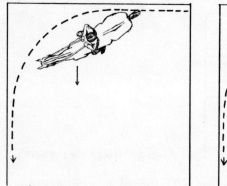

Fig. 9. Falling in

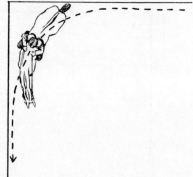

Fig. 10. Falling out

If a circle is attempted it will become an ever-decreasing spiral. This fault must be corrected at the walk first, and later at the trot. Working in a large circle, put the whip in the inside hand to reinforce the inside leg; ask the horse for the bend (just enough to see the back of the eye will do) and then insist that the horse keeps the bend. The horse will soon know what is wanted, and continued correct bending will supple the spine. One-sidedness will gradually disappear.

At the same time the rider must avoid too much use of the inside rein; if the neck is pulled round too far to the inside, the quarters will tend to "fall out" instead of following the front legs.

An aid to this exercise is to put an oil drum or other marker near the corner, thereby giving the horse something to avoid. This will correct the tendency to fall in. The marker can gradually be put deeper into the corner as the horse gets more supple.

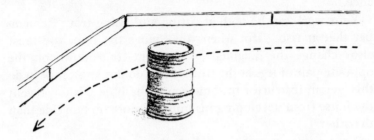

Fig. 11 Marker as an aid to riding the corner

Ride as close to the boards as possible, keeping the horse straight. A bad fault is to allow the horse to carry his "quarters in"; this fault is especially liable to occur at the canter. It is preferable to ride very slightly "shoulder-in," but this is a later refinement, not to be considered yet. At the moment concentrate on absolute straightness.

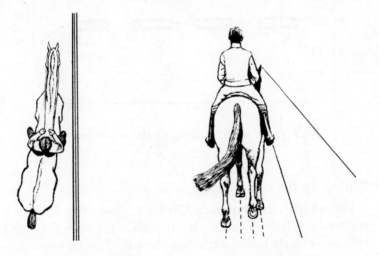

Fig. 12. Riding with quarters in. A bad fault

Try to ride straight on the short side as well as the long as soon as the horse can go into the corner without losing balance.

Your work can be both at sitting and rising trot. Remember that at rising trot when you change the rein, you must also "change the diagonal," — rise and come down on the opposite pair of legs at the trot. If you do not know how to do this, get an instructor to show you. The object is to prevent the horse from developing his muscles more on one side than the other.

Next, you may start to teach the horse to go straight up the center line. This is surprisingly hard to do, and impossible without some sort of guide. Either mow a straight line up the center, or else put pairs of boards about one yard apart, at D, X, and G.

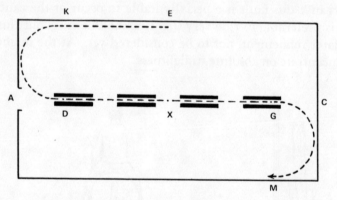

Fig. 13. Aids to riding up the center line

Riding up the center line

On the left rein, approach K from E. Just after K make a perfect half-circle of just under 10 meters diameter; this will take you exactly into the two boards at D. If your horse puts his head down to look at the boards, so much the better. Now fix your eyes on C and ride straight to G, where you can make a half-circle right to M. If you work with boards, your horse will get the habit of going straight. Practice walking as well as trotting on the center line, and halting between the boards.

"Overshooting" the center line is a bad fault, as is "wandering" or being "off-line." All will lose you marks in a test. Do not try to do this exercise at the canter yet, because the half-circle at the end is too small for a novice horse.

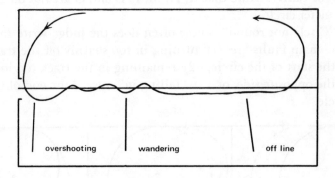

Fig. 14. Faults on the center line

Circles

We will now consider the riding of circles.

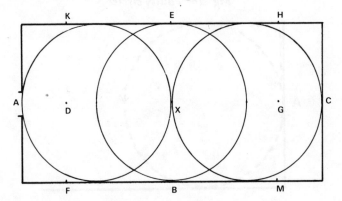

Fig. 15. 20 meter circles in the small arena

The circles for early tests will be of 20 meters — the full width of the arena. They will start and end either at A or C, B or E. In the small arena, circles from A and C pass through X and touch the track 4 meters from the "diagonal markers." The circles from B or E touch the track at the opposite marker and cut the center line exactly halfway between X and the short side. Twenty meter circles may be ridden at trot or canter. Note that K, H, M, F, D and G are *not* on any 20 meter circle.

"Circle not round" — how often does the judge write this! The main faults are (1) turning in too sharply off the track at the start of the circle, (2) remaining in the track too long at the opposite side, or (3) "falling in" toward the end of the circle.

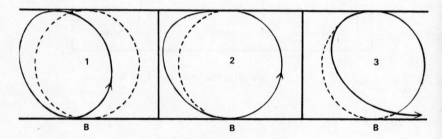

Fig. 16. Faulty circles

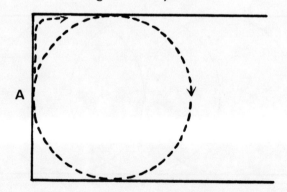

Fig. 17. Cornering after the circle

"Circle too small" speaks for itself and is another common fault. After riding a circle beginning and ending at A or C, remember to go straight on into the corner, rather than making yet another quarter of a circle.

Ten meter half-circles may be performed at the walk or trot by novice horses. A 10 meter half-circle should end exactly on the center line facing the end marker.

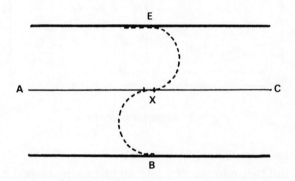

Fig. 18. 10 meter half-circles

Above: Linked 10 meter half-circles. Note that at X the rider takes one or two strides straight *on* the center line. Remember that the center line is 10 meters from the long side; circles of 15, 8, 5 meters may be required in later tests.

Serpentines and loops

These figures are generally shown in diagrams on the back of the test sheet.

The commonest are:

1. Linked half-circles of 20 meters, AX-XC.
   Note that at X the rider should face exactly toward B
   or E, and ride straight on the BE line for a horse's length.

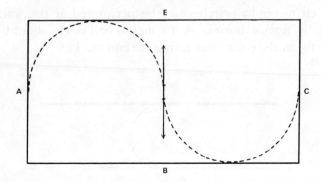

Fig. 19. 20 meter half-circles

2. Serpentine three loops, A to C.
   A difficult movement. The middle loop meets the track
   exactly at B, the outer loops half a meter from K and H,
   and cut the center line at one-third and two-thirds of
   the total length. The loops are *not* perfect half-circles.
   Loops must be exactly equal.

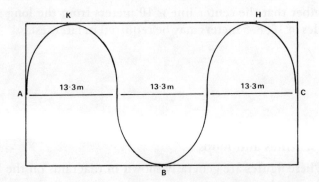

Fig. 20. Serpentine, three loops

3. Serpentine of three, four, or more loops each side of center line — depth of loops to be given in meters. Loops must be equal.

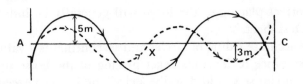

Fig. 21. Serpentine each side of center line

4. Loop K to H on long side, depth given in meters.

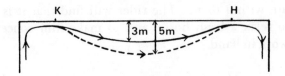

Fig. 22. Loops on long side of arena

These last serpentines are ridden without changing leg at the canter. The horse must keep the bend over the leading leg.

Serpentines and loops must be ridden with meticulous attention to the correct bend; the rider must keep the horse balanced when changing rein, and "change the diagonal" if at rising trot. There must be no loss of rhythm, nor change of speed. One must get the impression that the horse, having accepted the correct bend from hand, seat, and leg aids, will then continue indefinitely in that curve until the aids are changed.

Riding in a curve with the wrong bend is a very bad fault and will ensure that in a test the marks will be no better than insufficient. From the point of view of schooling the horse, allowing a wrong bend is merely failing to take the opportunity to supple the horse, thus permitting him to reinforce a bad habit.

Serpentines in the large arena demand less from the horse. The correct placing of the loops will generally be indicated on the test sheet.

The accurate riding of circles and serpentines is a valuable exercise, since it demands exact placing of the horse by the rider — no horse would describe a circle on his own except by chance. The acceptance of the bend has a suppling effect on the neck and back, and leads naturally on to the next phase in the horse's training — accepting the bit, with flexion at the poll and correct engagement of the hocks.

Riding in the arena creates a "sense of space" in the horse; he will soon start to accept the boundaries and to be content to remain within them. The rider will find that it is much easier to relax a fresh horse, and to make him concentrate on the work in hand.

Chapter 4

Impulsion

THE POWER UNIT OF THE HORSE is in the hindquarters. When on the move the front legs, like spokes of the wheel of a wheelbarrow, support much of the weight, while the propulsion comes from behind.

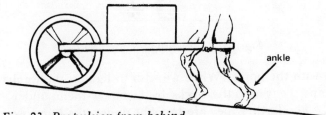

Fig. 23. Propulsion from behind

The ankle joint of the human being is the hock joint of the horse, the human toes being fused together in the foot of the horse. (In the human arm, the wrist is the equivalent of the horse's knee.)

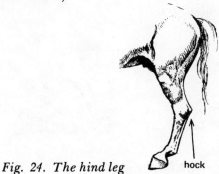

Fig. 24. The hind leg

Our general definition of dressage speaks of "lightness of the forehand and engagement of the hindquarters." If our man with the barrow wanted to lift the front wheel off the ground, he plainly could not do it by holding the extreme end of the shafts; he would move forward as far as he could to get his legs as much under the barrow as possible, crouching to get as much leverage as he could from his back muscles.

Fig. 25. Lightening the forehand

So with the horse. When we wish to lighten the forehand we must "engage" the hocks by bringing them under the body. The farther they are brought under, the more weight the hind legs can support, until in the extreme case, the *levade*, the whole weight is taken upon the hind legs, with the hocks flexed and the quarters lowered to half their normal height from the ground.

Try this experiment: get down on all fours with hands well stretched out in front of you.

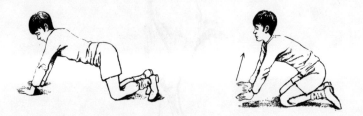

Fig. 26. Engaging the quarters

Now try to lift both hands at once from the floor without swaying back; it is impossible, until you bring your knees gradually forward under your body. Your hands will slowly become lighter, and at a critical moment it will become possible to lift them. A minute adjustment of balance the other way, and down they will go again. When you reach the critical point, try the effect on the balance of raising or lowering your head and leaning forward or back.

This is what is meant by the phrases "hocks out behind," "horse going on the forehand" (i.e., too much weight on the forehand); "hocks not engaged." Naturally the picture is more complicated when the horse is moving. The action of bringing the hocks under the horse, thus shortening his "wheelbase," is the most important part of the process known as "collecting the horse." In addition the weight on the forehand can be reduced by raising the horse's neck, thus "collecting" him at both ends.

There is no better illustration of this principle than Müseler's famous diagram, which he calls the "Principle of Collection and Erection." Modern translators would prefer the term "Collection and Elevation"! The series of pictures on page 28 is an adaptation of his drawing.

The effect of shortening the neck is automatically to shorten the stride of the front legs — some consider that a horse cannot put his fore foot *on the ground* farther than a point vertically below his nose — (though he can, however, extend it in the air).

The effect of lowering the quarters and flexing the hocks is to give bounce and elevation — known as "cadence" — to the stride. Thus we see that at collected paces the horse will take a shorter and more elevated stride, though he can, and should, maintain the same rhythm.

The other effect of collection is to store energy within the frame of the horse, exactly in the same way that energy is contained in a compressed spring. The rider then has the power to release this energy for an extra effort, such as the

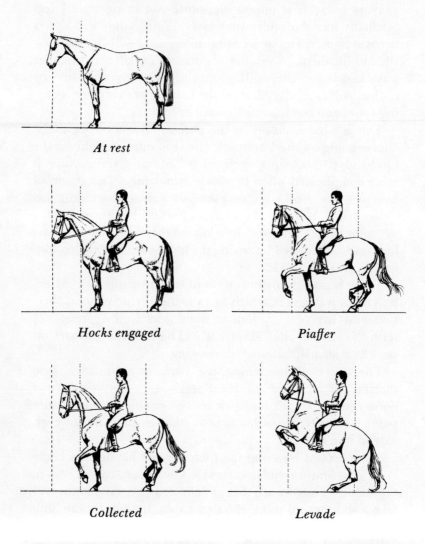

At rest

Hocks engaged

Piaffer

Collected

Levade

Fig. 27. Collection and Elevation. Note how, as collection is increased, the hocks are brought farther under the body and flexed to lower the quarters. The neck is raised until eventually the forehand leaves the ground.

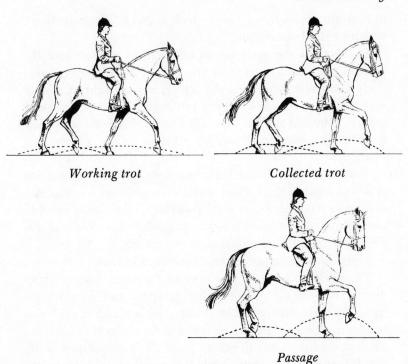

Working trot   *Collected trot*

Passage

Fig. 28. Collection at the trot. Note how as collection is in-creased the stride becomes shorter and higher, while the horse's neck is flexed more and slightly raised.

extended trot, a jump, sudden acceleration, or even such fantastic "airs above the ground" as the *capriole*.

Now for a word of warning — collection imposes a great strain on the muscular system of the horse — *and it cannot be achieved until the proper muscles have been developed.* Look back at the requirements of different standards of dressage, and observe that collection is not required until the Third Level test. *It is not for the novice horse, nor for the novice rider.*

The degree of collection attainable depends on the muscular and mental development of the horse. The novice rider should aim at nothing more than a good "working trot," which we shall soon define.

The aim in the early stages of dressage is to restore the natural grace and balance of the horse, which we have partially paralyzed by putting the tremendous weight of a rider and saddle on his back. Have you ever tried to ski or skate with a 30-pound rucksack on your back? It destroys all pleasure in the sport until you have practiced for a very long time.

Turn a common horse loose in a field with his companion and watch them float about like thoroughbreds in extended trot and even *passage,* in total contrast to the plodding dullness of their paces when you are on their backs. Yet it is possible to regain this freedom by correct training.

The proper sequence of training events follows:

The horse on his own produces his "natural" paces. Introducing the weight of the rider hampers and inhibits the natural paces, which must be restored by persuading the horse to return to his original free forward movement. This must be done by increasing the drive from the hindquarters, without hampering the horse with the reins. At this stage the horse's neck should be stretched out and down, "looking for the bit." The rider can then begin to establish the "working trot" — fully defined by F.E.I. as a pace ". . . in which a horse, not yet ready for collected movements shows himself properly balanced, and with a supple poll, remaining on the bit, goes forward with even elastic steps, and good hock action. The expression 'good hock action' does not mean that collection is a required quality of working trot. It only underlines the importance of an impulsion originated from the activity of the hindquarters."

Until the working trot is established, the horse is not ready for a test at any level.

At Training Level the gaits required are medium walk, working trot and canter, and free walk. (Note that there is no "working walk.")

At First and Second Level, medium and free walk are required with working trot and canter, and lengthened strides in working trot and canter. Change of leg at the canter is performed through the trot.

At Third Level and above, working gaits are discarded in favor of collected, medium, and extended trot and canter.

In Great Britain the above requirements are less clearly defined. In Elementary tests, the equivalent of Second Level, the rider may be required to show all four different paces — collected, working, medium, and extended — with resultant problems for judge and rider. But the rationalization of British tests is proceeding gradually, since the timely abolition of the misleading term "ordinary" trot and canter, which in Great Britain had for years been wrongly applied to both medium and working paces.

Our efforts to "engage the hocks" and "lighten the forehand" will therefore not be devoted as much to collecting and shortening the horse as to increasing the power coming from the hindquarters of the horse, and to lengthening the stride of the forelegs by extending the horse's neck and improving the movement of the shoulder. The horse's shoulder is not a solid joint — the shoulder blade is plastered to the rib cage by muscle and fiber. Therefore its movement, by proper work, can be improved.

We now have the key to the correct attitude for the novice horse, the goal toward which we must work.

First, active hocks, brought well forward under the body.

The leading leg is brought well forward under the body. The sole of the trailing foot should only be visible for an instant.

If the power unit is working well and the horse is relaxed the pelvis will rotate slightly, giving what is called a "swinging back." This will be shown in the movement of the tail, the end of which will swing like a tassel at the walk and trot.

Second, a long neck, with the face slightly in front of the vertical.

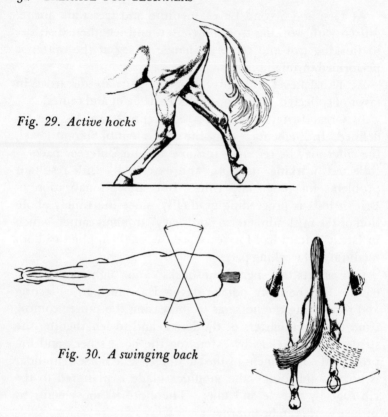

Fig. 29. *Active hocks*

Fig. 30. *A swinging back*

Fig. 31. *Action of the tail, showing a swinging back*

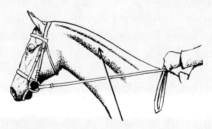

Fig. 32. *A good attitude for a novice horse; when the horse is going well, the muscle arrowed will be prominent, and will contract and expand in time with the stride*

The whole relaxed, yet lively and active.

Fig. 33. When asked for extended pace, the neck should go slightly out and down

Some common faults illustrated:

Fig. 34. Above the bit. *Rider trying vainly to pull horse's head down. Legs pushed forward in the stirrups accentuate the tendency of horse to pull against the rider.*

Fig. 35. Overbent, pulling. *Horse leaning on the bit.*

Fig. 36. Ewe neck, hollow back. *Stride very cramped, horse tending to "trample" up and down, rather than going forward.*

Fig. 37. Behind the bit (or over the bit). *Attitude similar to overbending, but the horse drops the bit intermittently, and the reins go slack.*

Fig. 38. Running. *The horse pokes its nose, kicks the soles of the hind feet out backward, and hurries; all the weight is on the forehand. Produced in a mistaken attempt to lengthen the stride at the trot.*

Fig. 39. Broken neck. *Flexion too far behind the poll. Though so-called, it has probably little to do with dislocated vertebrae, but is a wrongly developed muscular formation caused by forcing the horse into flexion too early in its training.* Fig. 40. Mouth open. *Shows lack of relaxation and non-acceptance of the bit. Ears laid back, unwillingness or resistance. In this case, the bit is too low in the horse's mouth, causing discomfort.* Fig. 41. Tongue protruding. *The tongue has probably got over the bit — a bad fault and difficult to cure; generally caused by rough hands in the early stages. If the tongue protrudes for short periods, without being over the bit, the fault is not so serious. The trouble may be due to insufficient room for the tongue under the bit.*

Fig. 42. Tilted head. *Horse resisting on one side, often caused by faulty teeth, or by the hand influence being stronger than that of the seat and leg.*

Crossing the jaw. *The lower jaw is pushed sideways, a certain sign of resistance.*

Fig. 43. Tail tucked in and dead. *Lack of energy.* *Fig. 44.* Tail high. *Often goes with "hollow back." Some breeds, notably Arab, have high tail carriage as a natural characteristic.* *Fig. 45.* Tail swishing. *Resistance.*

Fig. 46. Croup high. *A horse with stiff hock action at the canter carries its croup high and appears to be cantering down hill, instead of flexing the hocks and lowering the quarters.*

Fig. 47. Wide behind. *Generally caused by pushing the horse beyond its capabilities in an effort to lengthen the stride at the trot. Young racehorses often gallop wide behind, through being asked to gallop before the canter is properly established.*

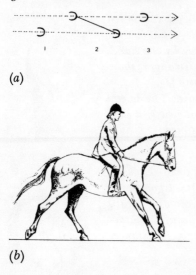

(a)

(b)

Fig. 48 (a), 48 (b). Four-time canter. The sequence of foot-falls for a horse cantering, as below, near fore leading, is: off-hind, right diagonal, near-fore, giving a beat of one-two-three.

If the horse loses balance, the rhythm breaks up, and the two feet of the diagonal do not strike the ground simultaneously, thus producing four beats.

Note this illustration does not show the fault, only the moment at which both legs of the right diagonal are coming to the ground.

The problem for the beginner will be how to persuade the horse to carry his head in the correct position. The young un-broken horse will very often have a natural head carriage and will soon adopt the right attitude; but the "spoilt" horse will have developed wrong habits and wrong muscles.

The art of getting a horse to flex correctly is not easily learned; the first thing to realize is that it is not done by the hands. You can sit all day on a horse, trying to pull the head down with the reins, and the horse will merely pull back at you — this will make things worse, since you are exercising the "pulling" muscles and developing them still further. Flexion comes from behind and can be produced by the rider's leg. Try the experiment of halting the horse, resting your thumbs on his neck, and then taking a steady but light contact on both reins *without pulling.* Now gently fold your legs round the horse with soft inward (not backward) impulses. If the horse tries to move forward restrain him with the reins and use the legs less strongly; gradually he will start to dip his head lower. When he does so, reward him by encouragement of voice, a pat, and lightening the contact.

If he tries to snatch the rein from you, hold firm, but do not pull. Let the horse feel he himself is making the discomfort by coming up against an unyielding bit.

Although this is not the correct way of getting true flexion — since it is done at the halt and not on the move — it will show you that flexion comes from a steady hand, accepting and controlling the impulse from the leg. Any unsteadiness of hand will cause movement of the bit in the horse's mouth, which will at once cause him to lift his head. Try shaking a rein if the horse's head is too low, and the effect will be to raise the head at once.

Our aim now is to get the horse to extend his head and neck forward and downward — no matter if it is too low at first, provided that rhythm and tempo are maintained. The sequence of training so far has therefore been:

1. Relax the horse.
2. Get free forward movement — straight.
3. Teach the horse to bend on curves.
4. Persuade him to lower his head and extend the neck, "looking for the bit."
5. Increase the power from behind and the engagement of the hocks to lighten the forehand and raise the head again.
6. Tactfully persuade him to flex at the poll by riding him into the bit from behind.
7. Lastly, train him to maintain this attitude at all times — especially during changes of direction and transitions from one pace to another.

This can only be achieved by the most delicate balance on the part of the rider, who must sit still, neither bumping the horse's back, nor wobbling sideways or back and forward. The rider's spine must be as carefully balanced in the vertical plane as a pile of wooden bricks; his hands must be as steady as though holding two glasses of water, his legs softly encouraging the forward movement. Hence the importance of a correct seat, which "follows" the horse's movement and keeps the rider's balance over the horse's center of gravity.

If you find yourself bumping at the sitting trot, try holding the front arch of the saddle and pulling yourself down into it. At once the bumping will decrease — you will be "going with the horse" instead of against him. It is this harmonious contact between horse and rider that is the essence of good riding. A horse with hocks engaged, and back swinging, will be far more comfortable to sit on than one with a high head and hollow back on which the rider will feel as though he is sitting on a board.

Naturally, the path to success will not be smooth: the horse will find innumerable resistances, some of which will seem impossible to overcome. The rider can only seek expert advice. A knowledgeable person can often see at once what is causing the resistance — generally a fault on the rider's part — and can help the rider to correct the trouble.

Let us end this chapter headed "Impulsion," with some consideration of this elusive word, which has many meanings for different people. Some just take it to mean "energy," i.e., "lacking impulsion" meaning "lacking energy"; but energy alone is not impulsion — it must be *energy completely under control*. Impulsion does not mean "speed" — a horse may run fast round the arena, but completely lack impulsion.

Colonel Handler* preferred this definition: "A tendency to move forward with elasticity, originating from the haunches, flowing into a swinging back, ending in the mouth."

* Late head of the Spanish Riding School.

Chapter 5

Transitions and Halts

A TRANSITION IS THE CHANGE from one pace to another. At Training, First, and Second Levels the transitions are mainly performed from one pace to the next — walk to trot, trot to canter. At Third Level the horse is expected to canter from the walk or vice versa; and at more advanced levels we find transitions from rein-back to canter, extended canter to walk, and so on.

If you read any test and count the number of transitions, you will find them occurring more often than any other movement. In British Test No. 1 there are fourteen, and in U.S. First Level No. 1, fifteen, including the two halts.

It follows, therefore, that if the transitions are badly done, there are plenty of opportunities for losing marks.

Transitions are of two kinds — upward to a higher pace, and downward to a lower pace. The former are the easier, since the horse is being asked to go forward, whereas in downward transitions it must "come back" to the rider.

Transitions must be *straight,* no swinging of the quarters; *smooth,* with no loss of balance; *steady,* with the horse's head maintained in the correct attitude; *soft,* with no wrangling or resistance; and they must be *forward* — that is to say the horse must not be checked — and the *first stride of the new pace must be a full one.*

At Training and First Level, when a transition is required to the next pace but one — halt to trot, trot to halt — it may be made "progressively," that is to say, with a stride or two of walk intervening between halt and trot.

Upward transitions demand *instant* response to the leg in order that the transition be accurate and that the horse go immediately into the next pace.

Downward transitions demand the ability to "engage the hocks" and lighten the forehand, or the horse will lurch forward and pull at the reins.

If our man with the wheelbarrow wishes to apply the brakes on a hill, he must put his feet forward under the barrow.

Fig. 49. Putting on the brakes

So the rider, to check the horse, must first ride him a little into the bit to bring the hocks more underneath the body.

This action, preparatory to a downward transition, is called a "half-halt"; it should never be obvious to the spectator, but should take place unobtrusively and quietly.

Beginners are often bewildered by the fact that in order to *reduce* speed at the canter on a green horse, it is generally necessary to use the legs quite strongly in order to drive the hocks under the body.

Downward transitions cannot be performed smoothly until we have the ability to "bring the horse back" to us by engaging the hocks. Once the horse is going freely forward, bending to right and left and beginning to flex a little at the poll, we must work toward improving his suppleness in the vertical plane by asking for frequent increase and decrease of speed, engaging the hocks, reducing speed, and then asking for a longer stride once more. This work is better done in the open, rather than in the confines of the arena, where we lack the natural tendency of the horse to go straight forward.

At first the canter is likely to be too fast. When asked to reduce speed, the horse will fall into the trot, but gradually, as balance improves, so will the horse gain in impulsion. Then, quite suddenly, the rider will find that he is able to canter calmly and quietly, without difficulty, the horse holding himself in balance.

Once this stage is reached, transitions become comparatively easy. The horse will canter, without effort, from the walk, and will soon be able to walk from the canter.

When working in the arena, the rider must avoid performing transitions regularly in the same place. The horse learns to anticipate transitions more rapidly than any other movement, seemingly able to sense the rider's intentions, which are in fact telegraphed through hand and seat. Many tests are ruined by anticipation, especially in movements where after the walk the horse is asked to trot or canter. The rider becomes tense, the horse shortens the trot stride and starts to jog up and down, following with an explosive or crooked strike-off to canter.

The rider, therefore, when working, will do better to concentrate on the smooth execution of the transitions, rather than on the accuracy of their placing, thereby preventing the horse from anticipating where the transitions are going to be made. In a test remember that a good transition, early or late, will get better marks than a bad transition made right on the marker.

There is one movement, however, which does not suffer from anticipation — that is the lengthening of strides across the diagonal of the school at walk or trot. In most tests, the free walk and the lengthened strides or extended trot take place on the diagonal. If the horse acquires the habit of stepping out on that line, no harm will come of it. The rider can always restrain, but cannot always produce a lengthened stride at will. Horses have quite a sense of space and direction and will soon get into the habit of going a little more strongly as the rider turns on to the diagonal. A discreet click of the tongue, inaudible to the judge, will help matters even further!

The transition to the halt is very often done carelessly at the lower levels of dressage. The rider must realize that any crookedness, however slight, is liable to severe penalty. Most horses tend to swing the quarters to one side in the halt because the rider has not been careful enough to absorb the energy softly in the mouth. The result is that the quarters continue to try to move forward when the forehand is stationary; the quarters, having nowhere else to go, must move sideways.

An even more serious fault is fidgeting — the horse *must* remain still with all four feet, and stepping back is a particularly bad mistake. Inattention, looking about, or tossing the head up and down is also wrong. Horses must be taught the discipline of standing still when being mounted, and while the rider takes up the reins and adjusts stirrups or girth.

Lesser faults include not standing square, being slightly off line, resting a leg, not being on the bit, and the hocks being too far out behind.

The transition from the halt to walk or trot, generally called the "move-off," must be absolutely straight.

The halt is best practiced while hacking. The rider should, if necessary, halt hundreds of times until the horse understands clearly what is required.

The illustrations of halting in figure 50 show the correct method of riding downward transitions, and the effective use of the rider's back and legs in engaging the hocks.

The rein-back is not required in tests until Third Level standard. However, if the horse is to be ridden in the countryside where there are gates to be opened, the rider will be hard-pressed if his horse cannot rein-back.

The aids for the rein-back correspond with those for the halt. That is to say the horse is ridden into the bit from

Fig. 50.

Wrong method of reducing speed — horse pulling up on the forehand, rider's hands too low.

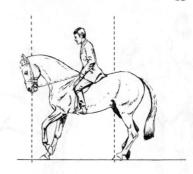

Correct downward transition, rider bracing back and using legs to engage hocks; horse's quarters are lowered.

Wrong again — rider pulling reins only, without using leg aid. Horse fighting and wrangling into halt.

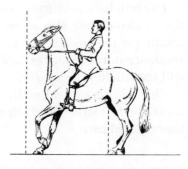

behind, engaging the hocks; the reins act persuasively, asking the horse to move backward, step by step. Pulling at the reins without leg pressure is wrong. The horse must keep his head still and move back without resistance for the exact number of steps required. Relaxation, straightness, and near two-time movement are the most important requirements. The horse should flex his hocks and thus lower his quarters. If the hocks

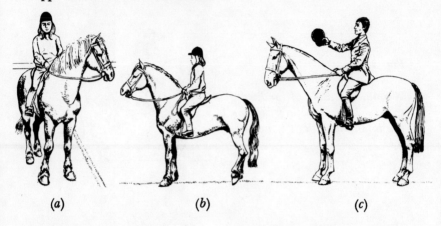

(a)   *(b)*   *(c)*

Fig. 51. Some halts illustrated. *(a) Off line, crooked, not square, inattentive — very bad. (b) Straight — but not on the bit, resting hind leg — insufficient. (c) On the bit, straight and square, good.*

are not flexed, the movement will throw weight on the forehand, and the horse will shuffle his forefeet along the ground.

The rein-back is valuable, not only as an exercise to lighten the forehand, but also as an indication of progress in the training of the novice. Any stiffness in the back, wrangling or resistance in the mouth or lack of ability to engage the hocks, will immediately be apparent.

The rein-back is normally followed by a forward movement, the first stride of which must be a full one straight into the required pace.

Chapter 6

Through the Judge's Eyes

THE JUDGE OF A DRESSAGE COMPETITION has the task of sorting as many as thirty or more competitors into an order of merit. In pure dressage the order is more important than the marks, but in Combined Training the marks are carried forward toward the aggregate total.

With such large numbers, the judge cannot rely on comparison, since many hours may elapse between the first and last starters. The judge must use absolute standards, comparing each candidate with the ideal. Naturally, the higher the standard, the fewer the faults; and at top levels the judge may penalize almost invisible errors which would be condoned in the lower standards.

A test consists of a number of movements, each marked out of 10, each mark signifying a standard. The scale is as follows:

10	excellent	5	sufficient
9	very good	4	insufficient
8	good	3	fairly bad
7	fairly good	2	bad
6	satisfactory	1	very bad
		0	not performed

(There is also a scale, out of 6, used in Three Day Events — 6 very good, 5 good, 4 fairly good, 3 passable, 2 bad, 1 very bad, 0 not performed.)

At the end of the test there are one or more headings for marks for general impression of the horse, and a final heading for marks for the position and seat of the rider and correct application of the aids. In the United States these marks are multiplied by a coefficient of 2x.

The marks are totaled, with penalties deducted for losing the way, using the voice, or (in some tests) going over the time allowed. From all this the final score emerges. In advanced tests some movements of particular importance are multiplied by a coefficient of 2x or 3x.

Beside each movement on the sheet is a space in which the judge can make remarks, justifying the mark; at the end the judge also remarks on the general impression of the horse and rider.

Riders sometimes complain when judges make a mark without comment, but they should remember that a mark represents a statement — "insufficient," "fairly bad" — and further explanation may not be necessary.

The judge must have a writer to whom marks and remarks are dictated.

There are, therefore, three ways in which horse and rider can gain or lose marks.

1. What the horse *is* — i.e., its paces, movement, carriage, suppleness, attitude, lightness, energy, muscular development, as shown in the basic paces or gaits, its acceptance of the bit and of the rider's weight and aids.
2. What the horse *does* — i.e., how well each movement is performed, and whether it is performed in exactly the right place.
3. What the rider is and does.

The first element is the most important and will set the general standard throughout the test; If the basic paces are faulty, the horse *must* receive low marks, however accurately it may go through the movements. Conversely a horse is unlikely to get marks of "excellent" or "very good" standard unless its general movement is also of this quality. A horse of this standard is rare.

In the detailed movements the judge will be looking to see that the horse maintains the correct footfall and rhythm through the movement, that it maintains its attitude through the transitions, and that it performs the movements not only according to the requirements laid down in the rules, but also at the right place. When a movement has to be performed at a certain point, it is when the rider's body is above that point that the movement should be executed.

In the third element, that of the rider, the judge will look for faults of position and exaggerated or wrong application of the aids. It is not always easy to allot these marks, especially when one is judging a good rider on a horse that is going badly, or when a rider, by apparently inelegant methods, is getting very good results.

Major faults will result in the loss of at least two or more marks — such faults being incorrect paces, uneven rhythm, unlevel paces, horse crooked, pulling, wrongly bent or stiff, tongue over the bit, overbent, above bit, etc.

Lesser faults vary with the stage of training, but include unsteady head, bucking, putting out the tongue, momentary loss of balance, inaccuracy, slight resistance, and so on.

The judge must look for the good as well as for the bad, must include praise as well as criticism, and, without attempting to act as a trainer, try to contribute something which will be helpful to the competitor.

The judge must be impartial, ignoring previous performances or knowledge of the horse, favoritism or prejudice for or against the rider.

There are other pressures too — the timetable, fatigue, and sometimes the presence of another judge who may be more cautious in the allotment of marks. Some judges are afraid to give very high or very low marks; when good competitors appear they become "crabby" and mark them down, and when bad riders come in, they feel sorry for them and are afraid of hurting their feelings. Judges must have the courage of their convictions, reward merit generously, and condemn the bad unmercifully. The medicine can be sweetened by kind remarks at the end.

Competitors should not be afraid to consult the judge after the competition, if they do not understand any remark; the judge's duty is to help the competitor.

All judges are different, and judging dressage is a matter of opinion and not of fact. Three judges, sitting at different viewpoints, may see the same movement in quite different ways and give varying marks. Some faults may go unnoticed by one judge, or may not weigh so heavily with him. In all sport, the competitors must submit themselves to the judge and accept the verdict in a good spirit. If the competitor thinks a particular judge is wrong, there is nothing to be done about it; but if a competitor begins to think that every judge is wrong, then it is time he looked into the mirror and examined himself!

Chapter 7

Riding a Test

BEFORE TAKING PART IN A COMPETITION, the rider must get a schedule from the organizer of the event. This document will tell the conditions for entry, the qualifications necessary, the time and place of the show, the date of the closing of entries, the time by which final declarations must be made, and a telephone number from which the competitor can ascertain the starting time on the evening before the show. Study the schedule carefully and note the details in your diary. A late entry may not be accepted, and failure to declare may involve loss of the entry fee.

Next, get a copy from the appropriate authority of the test to be ridden, and learn the test thoroughly by heart — but *not* by repeating it on the horse on which you are going to compete. It is essential to know the test really well, because if something goes wrong and you lose your concentration, you will find that the next movement has gone out of your mind completely.

When laying out your arena at home, remember that the judges are normally placed with their backs to the sun. If you are accustomed to orient yourself in this way, it may prevent confusion when you arrive at a strange arena.

Now you may practice the movements of the test, but do not on any account repeat the test in the correct sequence more than a very few times, or your horse will start to anticipate the next movement. Once this happens, it is very difficult to cure. Therefore, it is better to perform the movements separately, as part of your program of work, only fitting them together as a final check that you know the sequence correctly.

In most countries it is permissible to have a "commander" who reads the test out loud during the competition; such a "caller" is permitted in the United States, except in final or championship events, or in F.E.I. or Free-style tests.

When the day comes, arrive at the ground in plenty of time to "ride in," to get your horse accustomed to the strange place, and to get rid of any freshness or high spirits which may spoil the test. Report to the secretary and collect your number; "ride in," wearing your comfortable clothes, and put on your best kit at the last moment.

Find out the dress rules. To be either underdressed or overdressed is an error; the horse world is notoriously sensitive about correct clothing! Whatever the standard of dressage, good turn-out of horse and rider is an essential. Untidiness of either man or beast can only create an unfavorable impression with the judges, and though this *should* not affect the result, the loss of sympathy may also involve the loss of a mark!

The rules about spurs and saddlery are laid down by the national authorities.

Watch another competitor or two before your own turn; the steward will warn you when your time is coming. Generally, you will have been given a starting time. Sometimes the competition may be running a bit ahead of time — in which case you need not start before your allotted time — but if you are ready it will be kind to both judges and organizers not to keep them waiting. If your horse is not ready, then you may take your full time for preparation, but beware of insisting on taking your full time, only to be seen by the waiting judge gossiping with your friends rather than "working in." There may be another mark or two lost from lack of sympathy!

Walk quietly round in the collecting area while the previous competitor is performing. As soon as he finishes, ride round the outside of the arena to accustom your horse to the surroundings. The judge(s) normally sit in tents, horse trailers, small stands, or often at tables with umbrellas (in Great Britain, almost always in cars). In any case, the entire area may look very different from the familiar arena at home. When the judge is ready, he or she will signal by horn, bell, or whistle, and you must then go without delay to A and prepare to enter and start the test. Time allowed to ride the following test is five minutes.

We will now take you through First Level Test No. 1 on your cob,* "Conker."** This is the first time you and he have competed in a test in public. The test is in the small arena, the judge a visitor from England.

Test	Directive ideas
(1)	
A Enter working trot (sitting)	Entry (straightness)
X Halt, salute	Halt (immobility)
Proceed working trot (sitting)	Transition from halt

Conker feels straight on entry, but coming into the halt his quarters go out to the left. His head is still and the poll flexed. Now, salute: reins in left hand — hat off (man) or right hand at side with nod of head (lady). Take the reins, and off goes Conker before you are ready; never mind, hope the judge didn't notice!

Judge's thoughts — This combination looks quite business-like. The horse is on the bit; but the halt was crooked, and he seemed to anticipate the move-off. The trot is satisfactory, without being in any way brilliant or spectacular.

Judge's remarks — *Halt crooked, and not sustained: 4.*

* Cob — "big bodied . . . , short legged . . . , no higher than 15.3 hands with small quality head set on a neck arched and elegant." (Summerhays)
** Conker — the fruit of the horse chestnut.

(2)

C Track to the right

MXK Change rein, working
trot (rising)

K Working trot (rising)

Correctness, regularity, the flexion of the horse.

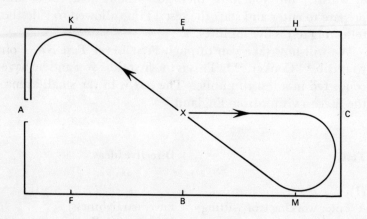

Fig. 52. Movement 2.

This is the first corner; at all costs show a proper bend.
Conker eyes the judges, ready to shy off and "fall in" round
the corner. Apply the inside leg, ease the outside rein, and
you are round quite well.

Now cross the arena, change your posting at X, and prepare
Conker for the next corner — aim a little to the right of K to
give yourself more room.

Judge's thoughts — Not too bad. The horse was a little stiff
in the first corner, but trotted nicely across the arena,
nearly worth 7.

Judge's remarks — *Nil: 6.*

(3)

A-C Serpentine in three loops
(width of arena)

Correctness and regularity of
the loops, the change of flexion,
and posting diagonal.

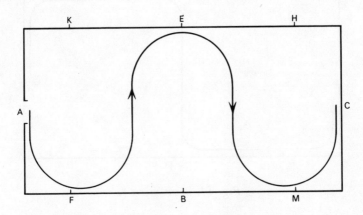

Fig. 53. Movement 3.

This serpentine is not an easy movement. Conker is a bit
stiff to the right. The first loop goes well enough; but in the
second he resists the change of rein, goes too wide, hits the
track after E instead of right on the mark, and as a result the
last loop is too narrow.

Judge's thoughts — I suspected the horse was stiff to the right
after that crooked halt, and this confirms it. He accepted
the bend better in the two left loops than the right. It
might have been worse; I may be a bit too kind.

Judge's remarks — *Not enough bend on right rein, loops
uneven: 5.*

(4)

E Turn left across centerline	Correctness, regularity, flexion
B Track to the right	of the horse

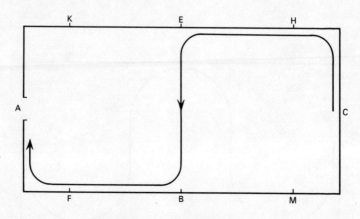

Fig. 54. Movement 4.

The turns must be ridden smoothly as small quarter-circles. As there is a change of rein involved, the rider changes the posting diagonal during the movement. In this case, the rider, thinking about the change of diagonal after the left turn at E, fails to prepare Conker for the right turn on his stiff side. He, therefore, falls round the turn with the wrong bend of the neck. Worse still, he does the same at F.

Judge's thoughts — This is really rather bad, two corners with wrong bend.

Judge's remarks — *Wrong bend at B and F: 3.*

(5)

A Medium walk	Relaxation, lengthening of the
KXM Change rein, free walk	stride and frame of the horse.
on a long rein	
M Medium walk	

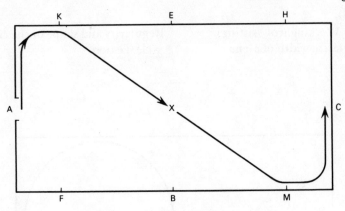

Fig. 55. Movement 5.

As a result of the stiffening in the corners, Conker is still resisting at the transition to walk at A. He sets his jaw and pulls against the rider, making the transition two strides late after A. Once into the walk he settles down and relaxes again, flexing the poll and coming down on to the bit. At K, when given the rein, he stretches his neck well out and down and walks out freely — one of his best characteristics. The transition to medium walk at M is crucial (we are going to trot at C and we must be careful that we don't anticipate the trot). Before reaching M, shorten the reins up very carefully *without* making contact; then at M try to bring the horse straight on to the bit with a half-halt. Don't overdo the aid or the horse will start trotting or throw up his head. In this case, all goes pretty well — we are on Conker's soft side (the left) and he accepts the bit kindly.

Judge's thoughts — Transition to walk was very resistant and late (take off one or two marks), but both medium and free walk are really good. Let's see if the rider can bring him back to medium walk without resistance — yes, he did it well.

Judge's remarks — *Walk transition rough and late. Free walk good: 7.*

(6)

C Working trot (sitting)   Regularity and shape of the cir-
  circle width of arena   cle, flexion.

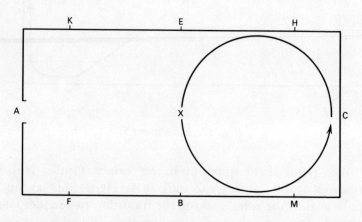

Fig. 56. Movement 6.

No trouble about this one; keep the circle full size, touching the track at the midpoints between the corners and E and B, and passing over X.

Judge's thoughts — Nice round circle, rhythm good.

Judge's remarks — *Nil: 7*.

(7)

C Working canter left lead, circle width of the arena once around, then straight on

The calmness of the canter depart, regularity and shape of the circle, the flexion of the horse.

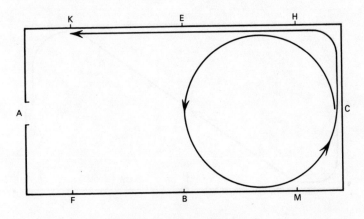

Fig. 57. Movement 7.

Conker strikes off well into the canter without throwing up his head. But his canter is a little too fast, and on returning to C he cuts the corner rather badly instead of showing a stride or two straight on the short side of the arena. Then when the rider tries to balance him for the transition to trot at K, he falls into the trot early and on the forehand.

Judge's thoughts – Typical of a rather green horse; canter unbalanced and on the forehand; too much speed without impulsion.

Judge's remarks – *Canter too fast and on forehand; fell into trot early: 4.*

(8)

K Working trot (sitting)	Lengthening of stride, mainte-
FXH Change rein, lengthen	nance of rhythm, the balance,
stride in the trot (rising)	the transition.
H Working trot (sitting)	

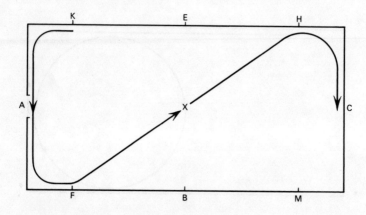

Fig. 58. Movement 8.

Pull ourselves together after that scramble, and balance the horse in the corners before changing the rein.

If we don't have some energy contained in hand before F, there will be nothing to give for the lengthened strides. Conker is not very good at lengthening yet, but we must try to show the judge a difference. So sit down and ride him into the bit between A and F, then after F release the rein and let him go forward. He does lengthen his stride, but, unfortunately, he hurries as well and loses his rhythm.

Judge's thoughts — There was some visible lengthening of the stride; it was a bit rushed, but he came back to the rider nicely at H.

Judge's remarks — *Slightly hurried: 5.*

(9, 10, 11)

These repeat 6, 7, 8 on the other rein, on which Conker is not quite so good. He gets 5 and 4 for his trot and canter circles; but in the lengthened strides the rider pushes him too hard, and he breaks into a canter and is marked at 2.

(12)

HXF Change rein, working trot (rising)	The regularity of the working trot.
F Working trot (sitting)	

Judge's remarks — *Nil: 6.*

(13)

A Down centerline	The straightness, the halt (immobility)
G Halt, salute	
Leave arena, free walk on a loose rein	The relaxation in the free walk.

Turning up the center the rider does not quite hit off the center line, and so passes to one side of X. However, the halt is straight this time, though the hind legs are not square. Salute, a smile for the judge in gratitude for his concentration on your behalf (and to conceal the fact that you are not very pleased with your performance), and walk out on a loose rein.

Judge's thoughts — Quite a good finish. A bit off line coming up the center, but the horse was straight, and relaxed nicely going out.

Judge's remarks — *Off line up center. Halt good: 7.*

Each of the movements above was marked on a scale of 1 — 10. The general impressions below are marked similarly and multiplied by a factor of two.

General Impression

(14)

Gaits (freedom and regularity)

Judge's remarks — *Natural paces rather limited, but rhythm quite good: 6 × 2 = 12*

(15)

Impulsion (desire to move forward, elasticity of the steps, relaxation of the back)

Judge's remarks — *Quite active and lively, but hocks not yet well engaged; canter unbalanced: 4 × 2 = 8*

(16)

Submission (attention and confidence; harmony and lightness and ease of movements; acceptance of the bit)

Judge's remarks — *Stiff to the right, otherwise willing and obedient: 4 × 2 = 8*

(17)

Position, seat of the rider, correct use of the aids

Judge's remarks — *Rider sits well, but not always using inside leg enough to ensure correct flexion or bend of horse in corners and circles: 5 × 2 = 10*

Total: 103 (Maximum Points Possible: 210)

Judge's thoughts: Without the coefficients doubling the collective marks the total would have been 82 for 17 items, just under an average of 5 for each item — slightly less than "sufficient" — a fair estimate in view of the horse's stiffness on one side; however, there were some nice moments — the horse has obvious potential, walks well (a good sign for the future), and, while he may never reach great heights, could do a nice test once the rider has overcome the stiffness on the right rein.

These American sheets don't leave much room for the general remarks on the collective marking, but there is plenty of space below to put something encouraging for the rider.

The winner got 140, and the worst mark was 73. Conker's performance makes him less than sufficient at present. But remember that performance in public and in private at home is a very different matter. Both rider and horse will be tense and nervous, and lapses of concentration may occur. By next time, Conker must be made more supple, and you must work to get his hocks more under him, so that he can canter a little slower. The judge liked his paces, and his walk — most difficult to improve — got the highest mark of the test. Many horses which can trot and canter well show a bad walk — so there is promise of better marks to come.

Work hard and constructively, and remember that "the amateur practices till he can do it right — the professional practices till he can't do it wrong."

Chapter 8

Conclusion

IT IS HOPED THAT THIS BOOK has given the rider some idea of
what the requirements of "dressage" are. It has always been
a matter of regret that we have no English equivalent for the
French word; to complicate the matter further, what has been
described in this book is called "débourrage" by the French —
a word with several meanings, including drawing the charge
from a loaded musket and polishing a young gentleman's
manners!

There has long been a feeling, which still exists in Great
Britain, that the whole business is nasty foreign trickery
calculated to "ruin a horse for fox-hunting." Doubtless it
would do so for the rider who hangs on by the reins, since any
horse with a good mouth will soon stop jumping for the rider
who sits back, gets left behind over every fence, and hits the
horse in the mouth with the hands.

However, the members of the show-jumping fraternity
have fully realized the importance of "work on the flat," the
term which they prefer to employ. No one nowadays can win
consistently against the clock over big fences with a horse that
is not supple, active, well-balanced, and submissive to the
rider.

The racing world in Britain stands rather aloof from
dressage, though some enlightened trainers send horses with
severe faults to be cured by dressage riders, and there are
examples of notable and consistent successes in the steeple-
chasing world by owners who have adopted simple dressage
methods in the early training of steeplechasers, before the

young horses have been put into the hands of the trainer. From the riding point of view a scheme for general riding instruction for apprentice jockeys has been well received by trainers.

Dressage in both Great Britain and America is in a healthy state, thanks to the efforts of the dressage committees of the national societies. The panel of judges is now selected, graded, and upgraded by examination; in Britain all judges are required to attend one or more annual conferences to keep in touch with current thought and new rules. In the United States judges must attend one standards clinic every two years. Failure to attend invites removal from the panel. These conferences, often open to riders as well as judges, do much to ensure that all judges are thinking on the same lines.

The beginner — or in fact any dressage rider — should try to attend one of these conferences or clinics, or to watch experienced instructors at work with their pupils, or to "sit in" with a judge at a test. Permission to do this is nearly always willingly granted and will not only help the rider to know the requirements but will also help him to understand the problems of the judge. In three or four hours of consecutive judging, demanding continual concentration, the judge has to make hundreds of rapid decisions, allot a mark, and make a remark (in justification for not giving full marks for the movement). The fact that the "remarks column" often contains more criticism than praise should not be taken as a personal insult by the rider, but is merely a reflection of the main problem with which the judge is faced — lack of time for anything but the essentials.

This book does not attempt to teach the rider how to ride. As said before, this end cannot be achieved by reading: there is no substitute for good professional instruction. We cannot teach ourselves to play tennis or golf, to ski or to swim, by the light of nature, without acquiring a fumbling and inefficient technique. The shortest cut to success in acquiring a skill is to learn a sound method distilled from generations of experience. Wrongly taught faults are desperately hard to eradicate, and it is better never to acquire them.

So, if parents want their children to ride well, then let them pay for the best instruction they can afford. Pony Club membership is within the range of all pockets. For the older rider, membership in a Riding Club may bring the opportunity for professional instruction which would otherwise be too expensive.

Any rider interested in dressage should join the American Horse Shows Association, which will give access to competitions, conferences, and the rule book, or one of the many local and regional dressage associations, affiliated with the United States Dressage Federation, in all parts of the country.

From day to day, the rider must compose his own program of work. At first the beginner may find it hard to "think of things to do." A regular lesson, say once a fortnight, from an experienced rider or teacher will insure that the rider is given something on which to work until the next lesson — the cure of a tendency to stiffness on one side, the improvement of response to the leg aid, "cavaletti" work to increase the flexion of the hocks, and so on. The rider will soon be able to use the arena, or the daily exercise ride, to the best advantage.

The great pleasure in dressage is that the rider becomes conscious that, in every step the horse takes, it is either done well or badly; and the rider can work positively all the time to improve the horse. Exercise no longer becomes a dreary chore, because at any pace the rider can be asking the horse to balance itself perfectly, to accept the bit, and to improve its suppleness and activity. The muscles of the horse will gradually begin to form in the right places, and the animal will become more beautiful, more tractable, and, incidentally, much more valuable.

Appendices

Glossary of Terms

Appendix 1

Making a Simple Arena

To make a simple practice arena — minimum requirements:
  13 wooden pegs about two feet long
  24 wooden boards — four to six feet long, four inches wide
     (17 are for the arena; remainder spare or to mark the
     center line for practice work.)
Put pegs to mark corners and letters (two at A). Drill ten boards at the end, remainder in the middle, and fasten boards thus to pegs with wire or string

Fig. 59. Method of attaching boards to pegs

Put two boards at each corner, one at each letter, and one each side of the entrance at A. For dimensions see page 12.

The letters may be painted on plastic buckets, cracker tins, etc., or if pegs are large enough, on the pegs themselves.

Mow the track and the center line for practice purposes.

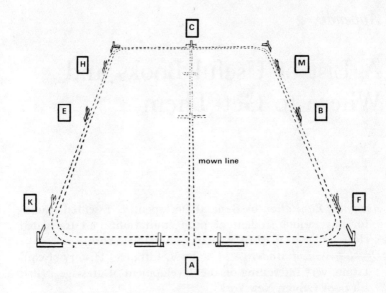

Fig. 60. A simple dressage arena

Appendix 2

A List of Useful Books and Where to Get Them

Academic Equitation by General Décarpentry. Essential reading for any serious student of pure equitation; well translated, clear, and logical. (British Book Center, New York)

Development of Modern Riding by V. Littauer. History of equitation, very interesting on the development of dressage. (British Book Center, New York)

Dressage by H. Wynmalen. Full study up to advanced standard, illustrations with photographs. (Arco)

Dressage Riding by R. L. Watjen. Full study, up to most advanced stages, and "airs above the ground," translated by Victor Saloschin. (British Book Center, New York)

Encyclopaedia for Horsemen by R. S. Summerhays. Useful compendium of riding terms with some illustrations. (Frederick Warne, London)

Equitation by Jean Froissard. Clear version of the French methods taught at Saumur. (Arco, Wilshire)

Fundamentals of Riding by G. Romaszkan. (Doubleday)

Give Your Horse a Chance by Lieutenant-Colonel A. L. d'Endrody. Full study, primarily for Combined Training. Author's meaning sometimes obscured by faulty command of English. (British Book Center, New York)

Manual of Horsemanship; Training the Young Pony; The Instructor's Handbook. Essential facts clearly stated. (United States Pony Clubs)

Olympic Dressage Test in Pictures by G. Romaszkan. (Greene)

Riding Logic by W. Müseler. Very clear study, admirable illustrations. (Methuen, London)

Riding Technique in Pictures by G. Harris and C. E. G. Hope. Helpful illustrations of right and wrong in many phases of riding. (J. A. Allen, London)

The Cavalry Manual of Horsemanship and Horsemastership edited by G. Wright. (Doubleday)

The Complete Training of Horse and Rider by Alois Podhajsky. Full study by former head of Spanish Riding School. (Doubleday)

The Trainers by Ann Martin. Interesting insight into the methods of training by leading British and foreign instructors. (Stanley Paul, London)

The World of Dressage by Neil ffrench Blake. International riders photographed in action with useful comments. (Caballus Publishers)

Glossary of Terms

Accepting the bit   The aim of the dressage rider, when the horse takes the bit willingly and softly, without resistance or opening the mouth.

Accepting the leg   The horse responds to, and yields to, the leg aid.

Accepting the weight   The horse's back swings softly, and the rider does not bounce.

Aids   Signals by which the rider conveys instructions to the horse.
(a) Natural   The hands through the reins, the rider's legs, the seat and balance, the voice.
(b) Artificial   Whip, spurs, etc.

Back   "Hollow back," a condition in which the horse's head is too high, and the hocks are out behind (see Fig. 36) .
"Rounded back," the opposite of hollow back, in which the neck is properly flexed, and the hocks engaged.
"Swinging back." A horse moving energetically and with a supple back is said to have a swinging back, which is reflected in the action of the tail (see Fig. 30) .

Balance   The adjustment of the weight of rider and horse to the best advantage.

Bandages   Are not allowed in tests.

Bend   Term for the lateral bending of the horse's spine and neck when traveling in a curve. See also "Flexion."

Bit, above, behind, over the   Faults, illustrated in Figures 34, 37.

Bits   Only two types of bit are allowed in dressage — the snaffle and the double bridle, as follows:

Training, First and Second Level — snaffle with either dropped or cavesson noseband.

Third and Fourth Level — snaffle or double bridle.

F.E.I. Levels — double bridle.

Variations of bit permitted are illustrated in *Rules for Dressage*.

Cadence   Rhythm with energy, which gives the pace an extra quality expressed by a springy and energetic lifting of the feet from the ground.

Canter   See gait and pace.

Capriole   A High School movement "above the ground" in which the horse jumps up and kicks out backward — not performed in dressage competitions of any standard.

Change of direction   Achieved by a turn or incline on the move.

Change of leg   To change the leading leg at the canter. In International rules "simple changes" are done by coming to the *walk* and striking off on the opposite leg.

"Flying changes" are performed by the horse changing legs in the air between strides at the canter.

Change of rein   To go round the school or arena in the opposite direction, or to change from one curve into another.

Chewing the bit   A good sign of relaxation and acceptance of the bit.

Collection   A shortening and elevation of the pace by collecting the horse "between hand and leg," bringing the hocks more underneath the body.

Contact   The contact of the rider's hands, through the reins and bit, with the horse's mouth.

Counter-canter   (Or counter-lead) To canter on the right rein with near-fore leading, or on the left rein with off-fore leading. The bend should be maintained over the leading leg.

Counter-change of hand A zig-zag movement, changing from a half-pass in one direction to one in the opposite direction.

Courbette A High School movement, in which the horse stands on his hind legs, with forelegs stretched fully upward. No part of any dressage test.

Croupade A High School movement in which the horse jumps vertically, the forehand higher than the quarters. Not used in tests.

Diagonal (of horse) Diagonal pairs of legs, i.e., off-fore and near-hind (right diagonal) and near-fore and off-hind (left diagonal).

Diagonal (of school) Corner to corner (K to M or F to H).

Disobedience Willful disobedience to the aids, e.g., wrong strike-off at canter, shying, bucking, etc.

Disunited Wrong sequence of footfalls at the canter; the front legs leading correctly, the hind legs on the wrong lead, or vice versa.

Extension A lengthening of the stride at the walk, trot or canter, to the limit of the horse's capacity, without change of rhythm (q.v.) or tempo (q.v.), or loss of regularity.

Flexion Yielding to the influence of the leg and the hand by flexing at the poll and relaxing the jaw. Also sometimes used to describe the lateral bending of the horse's spine. (See "Bend")

Footfall The correct sequence in which the feet come to the ground at different paces.

Forehand The head, neck, shoulders, withers, and forelegs.

Forging Clicking the hind shoes against the front; a fault indicative of fatigue, lack of muscle, or sloppy and unbalanced riding.

Freedom Free forward movement at all paces — the horse covering the ground with a long stride, willingly and without restriction of any sort.

Gait A term for "pace" (see also "Footfall"). The horse normally has three gaits: walk, trot, and canter. There are three more: the gallop, the "rack" (a four-time pace resembling a very fast walk), and the "amble" in which the horse trots with the off pair of legs and the near pair alternatively (instead of the diagonals). Neither "rack" nor "amble" are acceptable in dressage. Incorrect gait, e.g., cantering in four-time instead of three, is a very serious fault. The gallop is not used in dressage, except, when working in the open, as an exercise to free the horse's movement.

Half-halt The action by the rider of bringing the hocks under the horse in order to increase collection.

Half-pass Lateral movement in which the horse travels forward and sideways "on two tracks," bent in the direction toward which he is moving. The full pass, in which the horse moves sideways without going forward, is little used in dressage and never in tests.

Half-pirouette A pirouette through 180°, performed on the move at walk or canter, the horse maintaining the same rhythm and sequence of footfalls. (See "Pirouette")

Halt Bringing the horse to a standstill and remaining immobile.

Haute école or *High School* The classical art of riding, preserved in its highest form by the Spanish Riding School, Vienna. The culmination of High School riding goes beyond the most advanced stages of dressage to the "airs above the ground" such as Levade, Courbette, Capriole, and Croupade.

Hindquarters The structure of the croup, thighs, and hind legs providing the driving force for the horse's movement.

Hocks, engaging the Bringing the hocks more under the horse in order to be able to increase the forward thrust and to lighten the forehand.

Hocks, "out behind" The opposite of "hocks engaged."

Impulsion Controlled energy (Chapter IV).

Impulsion, lack of   Often indicated by loss of correct footfall in the horse's gait.

Jaw, crossing the   A sign of resistance, when the lower jaw is protruded to one side or the other.

Lateral movements   General term for work on two tracks; including leg-yielding, shoulder-in, half-pass, travers, and renvers (q.v.)

Lateral suppleness   See "Bend" and "Flexion."

Leg, rider's, inside or outside   The outside leg is that nearest the wall of the school or arena, or on the outside of any curve, e.g., on the left rein, the rider's left leg is the inside leg, the right leg the outside.

Leg-yielding   A lateral movement in which the horse moves forward and sideways, but is slightly bent *away* from the direction of movement (cp. half-pass in which the horse is bent *toward* the direction of movement).   Collection is not required for leg-yielding.

Levade   A High School "air above the ground" in which the horse lowers the quarters, with the hocks brought completely under the body, and raises the forehand off the ground. (See Fig. 27) Not used in any dressage test.

Martingales   Are not allowed in tests and should not be necessary for the dressage rider.

Mouth   Besides the actual mouth, the word is used to describe the horse's acceptance of the bit. A stiff resistant horse, with open mouth, pulling, is said to have "no mouth."

Neck, broken (See Fig. 39) ; *Neck, ewe* (See Fig. 36); *Neck, upside down* (See Fig. 1)   Faults in head carriage, caused by insufficient or incorrect training.

Noseband   Plain cavesson, or dropped nosebands, are permitted with a snaffle. A dropped noseband is not allowed with a double bridle. Crossed nosebands are now permitted with a snaffle bridle for combined training tests, but not in regular dressage tests.

Outline See "Profile."

Overbending When the line of the horse's face comes beyond the vertical. (See Fig. 35)

Paces (See also "Gait") The "basic paces" in dressage are walk, trot, and canter. The trot and canter are divided into collected, working, medium, and extended categories; the walk into collected, medium, extended, and free walk.

At First and Second Levels the horse is only required to show the "working" gait — with "a supple poll, maintaining light contact with the bit, going forward with even elastic steps and good hock action." At this level the horse is also required to lengthen the stride within the working gait.

"Medium" trot and canter require some degree of extension, while at "extended" gaits the horse must lengthen the stride to his full ability without loss of rhythm or hurried tempo.

In "collected" gaits the hocks are engaged more fully, the stride becomes shorter and higher, and the horse, storing energy like a compressed spring, becomes lighter in the forehand and more able to move in any direction.

Passage An advanced movement consisting of an extremely elevated trot with prolonged suspension. (See Fig. 28)

Piaffer An elevated trot in which the horse remains on the spot. See Passage. (See Fig. 28)

Pirouette A full turn of 360°, the movement being in fact a small circle on two tracks, the hind legs remaining almost on the spot, but maintaining the sequence of footfalls. Pirouettes are normally only seen at the collected walk, collected canter, and occasionally in piaffer.

Position of rider The seat and attitude adopted by the rider.

Position right or left The attitude into which the horse is put, with spine bent to right or left, in order to go round a corner. The horse can be ridden forward in position right or left as a suppling exercise.

Profile The outline of the horse seen from the side.

Punishment Can be by whip, spur, or voice, to show the rider's disapproval of a disobedience. Must be applied in such a way that the horse can associate it with the disobedience.

Quarters, in, out Hindquarters not following the front in the same track.

Quarters, lowering By flexing the hocks, the quarters are lowered, e.g., in rein-back.

Rein, inside and outside As for leg, inside and outside.

Renvers A lateral movement, half-pass with tail to the wall, the hind legs on the track, and the front legs inside the track. The horse is bent *toward* the direction of movement. Called "haunches out" in United States

Reward The expression of a rider's approval for a movement well performed. Can be by voice, patting, release from restriction, or by award of food.

Rhythm Regularity of footfall, at each pace, maintained whether at ordinary, collected, or extended pace.

Riding-in Preparatory work, before entering the arena for a test.

Ruade A High School movement, performed by the French School — the horse kicks the hind legs high in the air, the front legs remaining on the ground. (French also call this movement the croupade, q.v.) Not part of any dressage test.

Running An incorrect trot. (See Fig. 38)

Running reins An extra rein threaded through the ring of the bit, returning to the saddle. An extremely powerful weapon, capable of doing much harm, and forbidden in dressage tests. Also called "Draw-reins."

Serpentines Figures involving change of rein.

Shoulder-in A lateral movement, in which the hind legs remain in the track, and the shoulder is brought in off the track. The horse moves forward "on two tracks," bent *away* from the direction of movement. Requires some degree of collection.

Speed The actual speed of the horse, measured in miles per hour or feet per second. (See "Rhythm" and "Tempo").

Suspension A period in which none of the horse's feet are on the ground. Occurs at trot, canter, or gallop. (See "Cadence")

Tail, swinging A sign of good movement. (See Fig. 31.)

Tail, swishing or wringing A sign of resistance.

Teeth, faulty May lead to tilted head or uneasiness in the mouth.

Teeth, grinding A sign of resistance.

Tempo Rapidity or frequency of footfall, measured in time. (See "Rhythm")

Tracking up Or overtracking — describes how, at the walk, the hind foot should come down on, or in front of, the print of the forefoot on the same side.

Transition The change from one pace to another.

Travers A lateral movement, half-pass, head to the wall, tail in from the track, horse bent toward the direction of movement. Requires collection; called "haunches-in" in United States.

Trot, rising When the rider rises at each alternate stride. Called "posting" in United States.

Trot, sitting Always used for collected and medium paces, and unless otherwise indicated in all tests.

Trot, working Term for pace between medium and collected trot, in which a horse, not yet ready for collected movements, shows itself properly balanced; and with a supple poll, remaining on the bit, goes forward with even, elastic steps, and good hock action.

Turn, on the forehand A movement performed at the halt. To "turn right on the forehand" the rider draws back the *right* leg and applies it in order to cause the horse to move his quarters away to the left, pivoting on the off-fore leg, which should remain absolutely still. The horse is bent slightly to the right.

Seldom used in tests, but a valuable exercise for teaching the horse to move the quarters away from the leg.

Turn, on the haunches   A movement from the halt or medium walk in which the horse pivots on the inside hind leg, bent in the direction of the turn. Preparatory to the walk pirouette, which is performed from the collected walk.

Turn, right or left   A turn of 90° on the move, executed as a small quarter-circle, without loss of rhythm or balance.

Unevenness   Irregularity of rhythm or pace.

Unlevel   The horse dropping more heavily on a particular leg. Often used as a kind word for lameness, which term judges prefer to avoid. A serious fault; if it is very pronounced, the judges may order the horse to be inspected by a veterinary surgeon before continuing in a combined event.

Voice   A valuable aid, but not allowed during a test. Includes clicking of the tongue. Carries a penalty of two marks.

Volte   A very small circle, 6 meters diameter.

Walk   The various walks are as follows: collected, medium, extended, free walk on a long rein, and free walk on a loose rein.

Wandering   Deviation from a straight line.

Wide behind   A fault in action, illustrated in Fig. 47.